Reading Time

Juliette Saumande
d'après l'œuvre d'**Anna Sewell**

illustré par **Isabelle Mandrou**

relu et commenté par **Claire Béniméli**
professeure certifiée d'anglais,
chargée d'enseignement en ESPE

hachette
ÉDUCATION

A GOOD START

Hello!
Look at this young black horse:
it's me!

And this is Duchess,
my mother.

And this is my master.
His name is Farmer Grey.

I live in the countryside* in England.
The grass* is good. And my master
is a good man. People like to ride* on my back.
"You're a good horse," my master says.
And I'm happy.

One day, Farmer Grey sells* me to Mr and Mrs Gordon.

They're very rich. They live in Birtwick Park.

My new home is big and beautiful.

I have new friends: Ginger and Merrylegs.

"What a good horse!" Mrs Gordon says.
"Very intelligent! And very beautiful!
Let's call this horse Black Beauty!"

Now, I have a name, too!

FIRE! FIRE!

Today, Mr Gordon wants to visit a friend.
Joe, the groom*, prepares Ginger and me.
Let's go!

In the evening, we stop at a hotel. Joe puts Ginger and me in the stable*. He gives food* to me and to my friend. I am tired* so I sleep*. Suddenly, I wake up*.

"Look, Ginger!" I say. "Smoke*!"

"Fire*! Fire!" Ginger cries.

All the horses panic.
Suddenly, Joe arrives. He's very calm.
"Come, Black Beauty!" he says. "Good horse!"

Soon, I'm outside. I'm fine.
But Ginger is in the stable. She's terrified.
"Ginger!" I cry.
Finally, Joe finds my friend. The firemen arrive.
But two horses die* in the fire.

HARD TIMES

Mrs Gordon is very ill* now.

"Sunshine* is the only solution," the doctor says.

So the family goes away*. And Mr Gordon sells Ginger and me.

We have new masters: Lord and Lady W.
Lord W is OK. But Lady W is cruel.
"Quick! Quick!" she says. But I'm tired.
"Use your whip*!" she says to Reuben Smith, the groom. The whip hurts*.

Reuben is a good man. But one day, he drinks* a lot of alcohol in a bar. And he becomes cruel.

I have a stone* in my shoe*. It hurts! But Reuben doesn't see it. I want to stop, but he refuses. And he uses his whip.

Reuben and I fall*.

Rueben dies. And I'm hurt.

My legs are horrible now… So Lady W sells me.

I have a lot of new masters: good masters, cruel masters, intelligent masters, stupid masters…

Jerry Barker is an excellent master.
With Jerry, I go to London. I'm a cab* horse now.
It's dangerous, it's hard work. But it's exciting, too.

One day, Jerry is very ill. So he goes to the countryside… And he sells me!

At the market, an old man and a young boy look at me.

"Look at this horse, Grandad!" the boy says. "He's beautiful."

"Yes, Willie," the old man says. "But he's ill and tired, too."

"Let's buy* this horse!" Willie insists. "You're a great doctor of horses, Grandad!"

The old man accepts. His name is Farmer Thoroughgood. He is my new master now.

Farmer Thoroughgood and Willie live in the countryside. They give me food, love and tranquillity. After one year, I'm in good form. I'm happy, now.

One day, we visit Miss Blomefield.
"Do you want to buy this horse?" my master asks. "He's great."
"Maybe," Miss Blomefield says. "Let's ask the groom!"

The groom arrives.
"Incredible!" he says. "It's Black Beauty! From Birtwick Park!"
It's Joe! My old groom!
"Miss Blomefield," Joe says. "Black Beauty is an excellent horse. Please, buy this horse!"
"OK," she says.

And so I live here now. I have good grass, good masters and no work. I'm very happy!

Lexicon

countryside

grass

to ride

to sell

a groom

a stable

food

tired

to sleep

to wake up

smoke

fire

to die
ill
sunshine

to go away
a whip
to hurt

to drink
a stone
a shoe

to fall
a cab
to buy

Contents

hachette s'engage pour l'environnement en réduisant l'empreinte carbone de ses livres. Celle de cet exemplaire est de :

250 g éq. CO_2

Rendez-vous sur www.hachette-durable.fr

Édition : Pauline Gaberel
Création de la maquette : Estelle Chandelier
Mise en page : Cyrille de Swetschin
Fabrication : Marine Wiplier

ISBN : 978-2-01-118202-9

Achevé d'imprimer en Italie par L.E.G.O. S.p.A.
Dépôt légal : Janvier 2014 - Édition n° 01 - Collection n° 69
11/8202/1

ROY McKIE'S

ZODIAC BOOK

ROY McKIE'S
ZODIAC
BOOK
Collins
Glasgow and London

First published in this form 1977
Published by William Collins Sons and Company Limited
Glasgow and London

Printed in Great Britain
ISBN 0 00 410717 9

Aquarians are keenly interested in world affairs,

and learn well from others.

They tend to be impractical,
are self-appointed revealers of the truth,

and often have cold hands and feet.

They have an inventive genius,

are extremely independent

and are always eager to try something new.

They are tremendously likeable

but resent criticism.

Pisces people are not deeply competitive,

but are good in jobs requiring imagination.

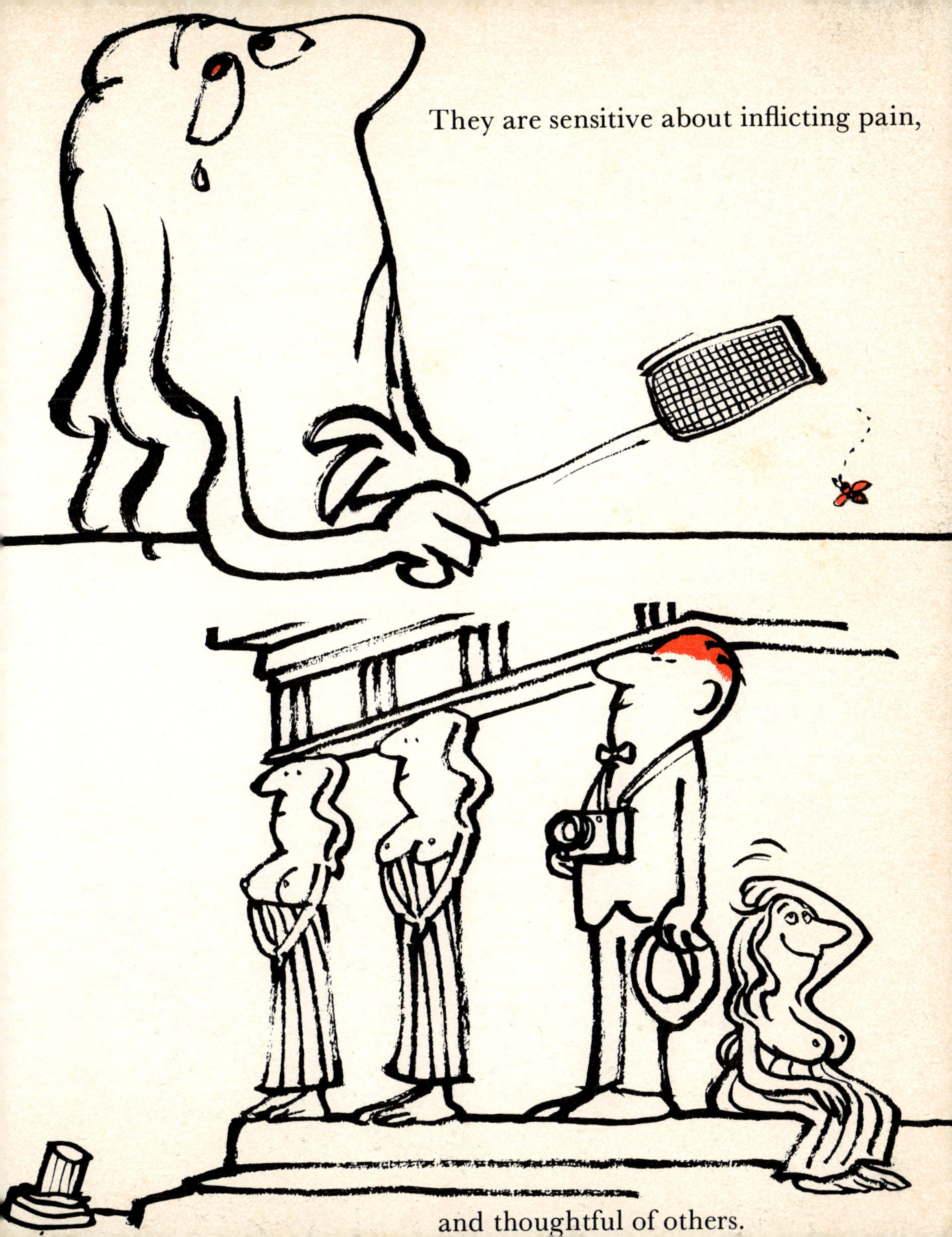

They are sensitive about inflicting pain,

and thoughtful of others.

They can be their own worst enemy,

make superlative crooks,

can be absent-minded,

and can become drifters.

They are adoring,

and lovable.

Aries people are punctual,

and make excellent military leaders.

They have firm hand clasps,

walk rapidly,

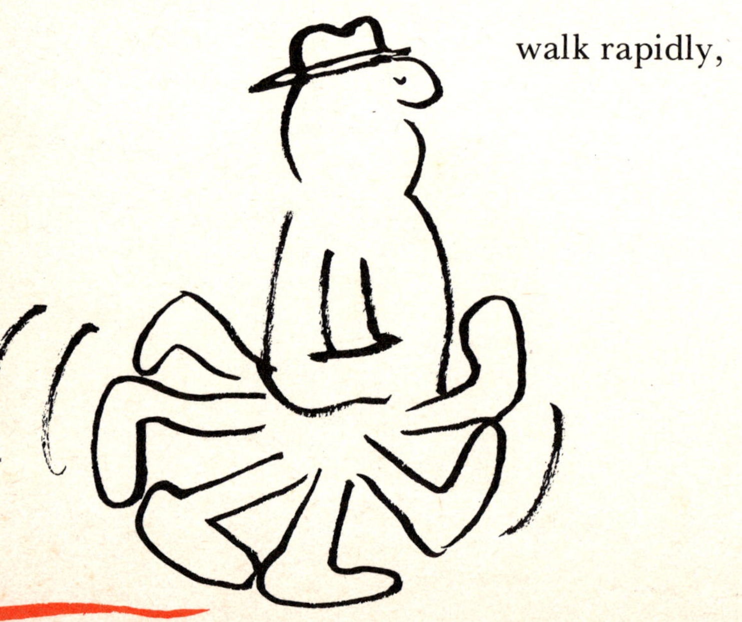

and are poor in subservient positions.

They are good at removing obstacles,

love to find the truth,

and are self-sufficient.

They enjoy life,

and they forget failure easily.

Taurus people are musical

and have a keen interest in the facts of life.

They are good at gardening,

apt to overindulge,

and they can be stubborn and pig-headed.

They are slow to anger

but can be bitter enemies.

They have an uncomplicated approach to sex

and their great warmth

makes them loved by all.

Gemini people have sex appeal,
Gemini May 22 to June 21
GEMINI
are witty,

and inventive.

They can't stand waiting

and their moods swing from one extreme

to the other.

They are flirtatious,

sparkling,

good salesmen,

and are apt to leave you with the check.

CANCER
Cancer June 22 to July 22
Cancer people are warm and friendly,
are good cooks,

and have a great interest in family history.

They follow the styles of the group,

are excitable,

and weep easily.

They are somewhat timid,

and like to be taken care of.

They love the sea

and are wonderful homemakers.

Leos are playful,

are good at delegating disagreeable duties,

and believe in their own superiority.

They like the sound of their own voices,

can be bossy,

peevish,

loyal,

and are poor judges of character.

They are pleasure-loving

and popular.

Virgos are hard workers,

quiet but good dressers,

and are calm and practical.

They have a tendency to hoard,

are worriers,

and have difficulty relaxing.

They are kind,

and always prepared.

They love pets

and are dedicated perfectionists.

Libras are graceful,

poor at scientific work,

and tend to be dabblers.

They frown on displays of passion,

and find friends everywhere.

They constantly seek balance

and are thorough housekeepers.

They excel in entertainment,

ke fancy clothes,

nd even in old age their love affairs are important.

Scorpios enjoy challenging problems

and love secrets.

Their responses are more emotional than rational.

They are brooders

and can be difficult to live with.

They have a lively curiosity

and a highly developed critical sense.

They are silent and strong-willed,

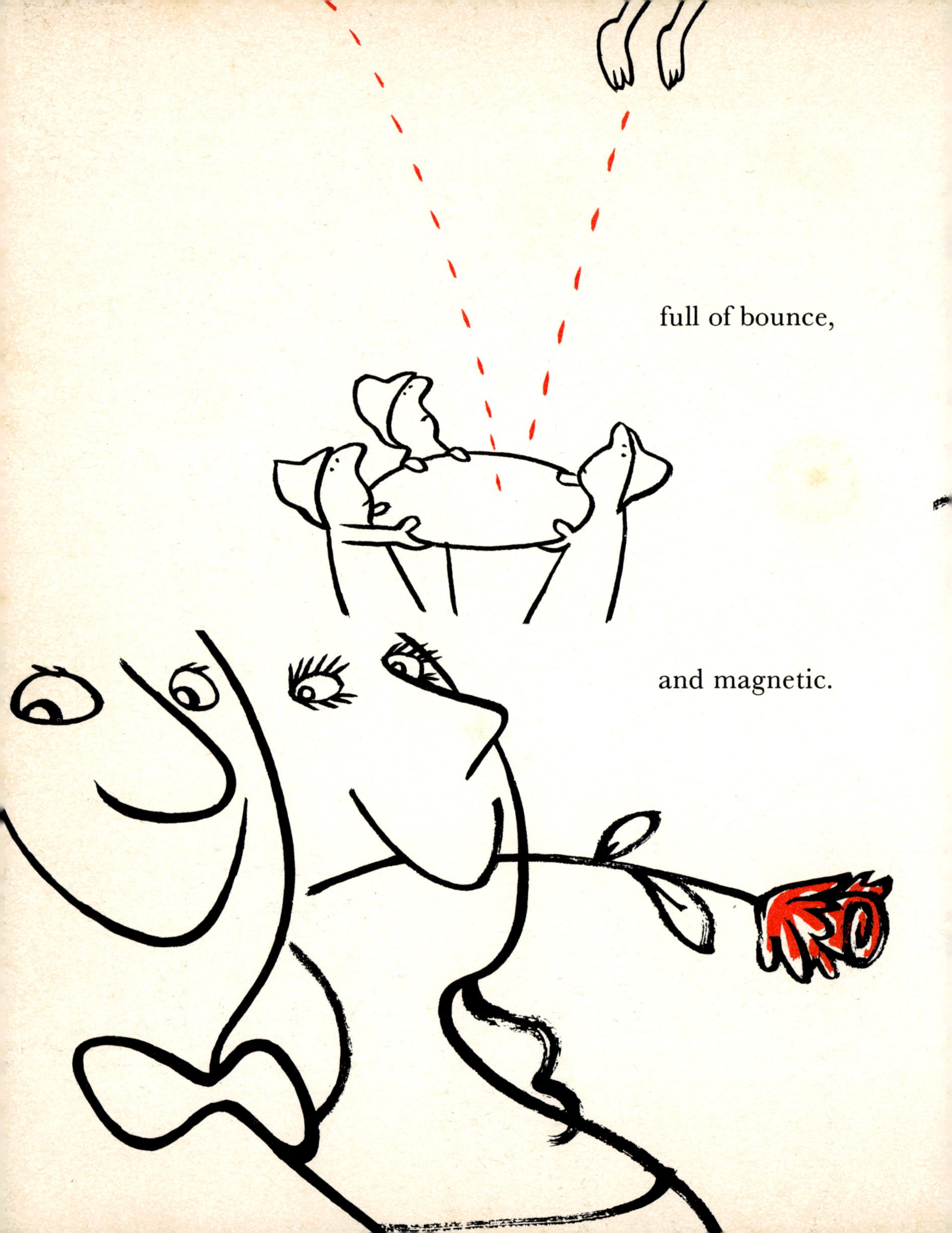

full of bounce,

and magnetic.

Sagittarius November 23 to December 21
SAGITTARIUS
Sagittarians are unpredictable,
impatient,

and inclined to preach.
They are often deceived by people.

They like to see wickedness punished
and good rewarded.

They tend to be impressed by position

and enjoy exploring foreign lands.

They are generous

and always good humoured.

Capricorn December 22 to January 20

Capricorns have a good eye for value,

are industrious,

ambitious,
and respond well to the security of a fixed routine.

They are somewhat shy,

can be despondent

and are completely honourable.

They enjoy solitude,

can be intolerant
and are eternally faithful.